MENTORS MATTER

MENTORS MATTER

Lessons for Aspiring Teachers and School Administrators

Dr. Edward Albert

Berry St Books
Lemont | Berlin

©2024 by Edward Albert
Printed in the United States of America

All rights reserved. This publication is protected by Copyright, and permission should be obtained from the publisher prior to any prohibited reproduction, storage in a retrieval system, or transmission in any form or by any means, electronic, mechanical, photocopying, recording, or likewise.

Published by Berry St Books, an imprint of Eifrig Publishing, PO Box 66, Lemont, PA 16851.

For information regarding permission, write to:
Rights and Permissions Department,
Eifrig Publishing,
PO Box 66, Lemont, PA 16851, USA.
permissions@eifrigpublishing.com, 814.954.9445.

Library of Congress Cataloging-in-Publication Data

Albert, Edward, *Mentors Matter: Lessons for Aspiring Teachers and School Administrators*
   p. cm.

Paperback:	ISBN 978-1-63233-397-1
Ebook:	ISBN 978-1-63233-398-8

   1. Education, 2. Educational leadership
   I. Albert, Edward II. Title.

28 27 26 25 2024
5 4 3 2 1

Printed on acid-free paper. ∞

*Dedicated to my biggest mentors in life,
Mom and Dad*

*Brixton and Tatum, these mentors shaped my professional world and helped me find success. I hope you have mentors in your workplace who do the same.
~Love, Dad*

TABLE OF CONTENTS

Foreword	9
Introduction	13
Dr. John Spears	15
Mr. Ira Light	20
Dr. William Starr	26
Dr. Lee Rhodes	31
Dr. Joseph McSparran	35
Dr. Woodrow "Woody" Sites	39
Dr. Jon Rednak	43
Mr. Joe Bard	47
Dr. Edward Albert	51
Other Individuals Who Played a Positive Role in My Success as an Administrator	57
Acknowledgments	58
About the Author	60

FOREWORD

Ed Albert is an authentic leader and has produced a book that takes you along on his professional journey in education. You'll get acquainted with the individuals he met along the way who shaped his style, work ethic, and his views about mentoring the next generation of educators.

My relationship with Ed had nothing to do with mentoring. In fact, we could have been antagonistic to each other during each encounter, but it never turned out that way. Let me tell you more.

I was hired by the Pennsylvania State Education Association (PSEA) in November 2007 after spending 10 years teaching elementary school in the Hamburg Area School District in Berks County, Pennsylvania. The job of a union is to advocate for its members. Many see it as mainly negotiating terms and conditions of employment, specifically salaries and benefits, but there is much more to it. By nature, people associate union/employer relationships as adversarial. Many times this is true, but it doesn't have to be that way.

My first assignment was to work with 14 local PSEA associations, all with different issues and populations of members. One of the local associations I was assigned to in 2007 was the Tulpehocken Education Association. The district and the Association had a long track record of contentious, drawn-out negotiations, including two previous strikes. The first meeting I attended was a bargaining session that was anything but amicable. The district "leadership" at the time had fostered a culture of disrespect and employees feeling undervalued. We persevered through the next two years, but the atmosphere in the district was taking a toll on the staff and made a very difficult job even harder.

In the fall of 2009, the district hired a new superintendent named Ed Albert. There was hope that he would be a change for the better, but the years of disrespect made it hard to believe that he could work that much magic.

During our first meeting with Ed, he said all the right things. Saying the right things is easy; actually doing those things is much more difficult. There was a level of optimism but still a lot of concern about how things would actually progress. After a few months, there was a level of respect and admiration being given to employees that had been absent for years. Ed got to know people on an individual basis and established relationships with them. This is a component of leadership that I feel is missing in education today but was key to altering the culture at Tulpehocken.

Ed held everyone accountable, which meant not blindly supporting administrators just because they were administrators. He expected people to work hard, and if someone wasn't, he'd address the matter.

Ed set high expectations for himself and, therefore, expected the same from everyone else. I remember being surprised when I learned that he sent an evaluation form to all employees for their feedback. That's something I haven't seen before, and it put him in a vulnerable position. The anonymous questionnaire landed in the mailbox of each district employee and went a long way to rebuild the trust that had been destroyed in previous years. The most impactful part of the survey was its aftermath. He took the feedback seriously and adjusted how he did things moving forward.

During Ed's six years in Tulpehocken we didn't agree on everything, but we did establish a working relationship that benefited the district and its personnel and students.

My definition of leadership is to design a set of behaviors used to help people align their collective direction, to execute strategic plans, and to continually renew an organization. I would add that a real leader will never ask their people to do something that they themselves wouldn't do. A leader motivates people by making them feel valued and important. They also know how to get the most production out of everyone's talents. Quite simply a good leader cares about people and the organization and will do whatever it takes to make everyone succeed. That's Ed.

~John McKiernan, PSEA UniServ Representative

INTRODUCTION
A Career—and a Book—Take Root

My long and happy life in education took root in Miss Blouch's kindergarten classroom in South Lebanon Elementary School back in 1959. It was there that I made a strong connection with my school and teacher and created a bit of a sensation, too.

Traditionally in kindergarten, students participate in several activities and routines throughout the school day. Snack time was one of my favorites, and frequently the teachers created craft activities from leftover milk cartons. After our cookies and milk Miss Blouch asked us to cut off the top of our milk containers to create little boxes perfect for planting. I remember scooping topsoil into the box and sprinkling grass seed on top. We placed the containers on a sunny windowsill, and I was excited to see the green blades of grass sprout and grow. My grass grew tall and thick and even until the day the bathroom line was too long. I waited. And waited. And since I was unable to wait any longer to relieve myself, I peed in my milk carton, killed the grass, and spent another year in kindergarten. Or so the story goes. I think I just loved kindergarten so much I was held back for a second year.

Although my education started with a small setback, the next five decades were filled with successes, graduations, employment, and job advancement. I spent 38 years as an educator, including seven as a teacher and 31 years as an administrator. During that time I was blessed with mentors who offered guidance and lots of expertise. After receiving my first administrative post in the Red Lion School District, it was Eugene McCleary, former administrator in the Cornwall Lebanon School District, who reminded me that God gave me two ears and one mouth. "So, lad, listen to advice from those with experience, and you will be fine."

I took McCleary's advice and listened. And just as he promised, I learned. The purpose of this book is to give recognition to all my mentors and share their wisdom with new and aspiring teachers and school administrators. Over my lifetime I've attempted to thank each of them, but the urge to express myself in writing and set down their stories and lessons is too strong to overcome. This small book of thanks is the result of the need to say and do a bit more.

From the bottom of my heart, I thank all my mentors—for their friendship, their wisdom and their encouragement. My life in education would not have been possible without you.

Dr. John Spears

They said it couldn't be done. Me? In college?

Back in 1973, my guidance counselor at Cedar Crest High School told me to find an hourly job after graduation. I couldn't really blame him. My grades were average—that's overlooking the four Fs on my report card during sophomore year that got me kicked off the basketball team. My SAT scores weren't too hot either. While I excelled at sports and navigating the social scene, I didn't set the academic world on fire. I generated a few sparks here and there, but going to college and studying education seemed as unlikely as me suiting up for my dream team, the Alabama Crimson Tide. I had an abiding love for the Tide, and in the back of my mind I thought I could be a walk-on sensation.

I never traveled into the deep south to meet Coach Bear Bryant, but I did find my way to West Virginia and Dr. John Spears, a political science professor and advisor who gave me my first real taste of success off the playing field.

I applied and was accepted to Salem College. I remember being so nervous my first semester because I had to maintain a 2.0 grade point average. I managed a 2.2 and thought I made Dean's List. It was a triumph, but I knew the second semester was going to be even tougher. I kept my celebration short because I had a political science course on deck with Dr. Spears, whose demands and high expectations were legendary among my classmates. He was well respected throughout the state by governors, legislators and fellow educators. He served as a campaign manager to former U.S. Senators from West Virginia, Robert Byrd and John 'Jay" Rockefeller. I always wondered why he wasn't at Harvard instead of little Salem College. No one ever got an A in his course, but I was not concerned about getting an A. I just wanted to pass.

One of our first assignments was to prepare for a classroom debate. I don't remember many of the details now, but each student chose a point of view and then stood up before the class to make his case. As the presentations began, my spirits sank. Everyone in class supported the opposite viewpoint from my own. By the time it was my turn, I was the only one to embrace the counterpoint. Each student spoke about academic achievement being the key to success while I extolled the virtues of hard work and interpersonal skills. I did my best but wasn't sure what my classmates or Dr. Spears thought of my argument.

On the way out of class Dr. Spears asked me to stay behind. His summons made me believe the worst—that I had failed. I was worried that my old pattern of academic underachievement was beginning to take hold in college, too.

To my surprise Dr. Spears told me that I did a tremendous job. At first, I thought he was sympathizing with me because I was the only person to advocate an unexpected point of view. But I was mistaken. Instead of another disappointment or another round of failure, Dr. Spears delivered a very different message that day. He told me that I had a gift and could become a very good student.

What a shock! Someone actually had faith in me. During this remarkable conversation, he asked me if I'd like to be one of his interns in the education department and help him complete his doctorate. I had no idea what I was getting into, but I was convinced that this professor was a positive influence. His trust made all the difference to me, and I immediately accepted his offer. It was one of the best decisions I ever made in my life.

Although I had an official advisor in the education department, John guided me through my years at Salem and provided plenty of individual attention. He held my feet to the fire and made sure I always did my best. He provided guidance, suggestions, and commentary on my work. Because of John, I worked very hard on my studies and made Dean's List—for real this time—during my last two years of college.

After I graduated from Salem, John and I stayed in touch. I remember him coming to my home in Lititz, PA one weekend to help me on a very important project. We sat at the dinner table from morning to night writing my thesis for Millersville University. There were many moments during that weekend when I just wanted to walk away and forget about the job before me, but he would not allow it. He told me that if you wanted something you needed to dedicate yourself to it entirely. And I did.

After graduation I became a teacher in the Cornwall Lebanon School District and remained close to John. As time passed, I expanded my professional goals and experiences. I began volunteering for the Special Olympics and obtained a principal certificate. With each milestone I always phoned John to share my good news.

Many years later my son was in a golf tournament in West Virginia, and we were able to reunite with John for dinner. Later, when I had an opportunity to write a grant for a paper company in Lancaster, Pennsylvania, I turned to John for help. With his input I wrote the grant, and the company received $100,000. John was among the first to hear the news.

On the day I received my doctorate degree, John was happier for me than I was for myself. His message never changed. He told me he was my mentor; he told me that I could achieve anything I wanted. Truthfully, I never tired of hearing those words from John. He lifted me up each time we met.

From that point on we agreed to have contact once a month, but as we got busy with our lives, time slipped away. While traveling home from a summer vacation, I thought I should contact John because it had been two, maybe three months since we spoke. When I finally found the time to call, he did not answer his home phone. That seemed unusual because John was always there for me. Then I called his office, and one of his colleagues answered.

"Where is John?" I asked. All I got was silence.

"Haven't you heard?"

"Heard what?"

John had suffered a fatal heart attack. I was devastated and did not want to believe the news. At that moment John taught me another hard lesson—never procrastinate. Deep down I knew I had the time to call John but pushed it off. There would be time later, I thought.

Had he answered the phone that day I know what I'd say. I'd tell John that he was the cornerstone of my educational successes and that I'd always be indebted to him for his support. I'd make plans to see him soon, and I'd express again that I'll be forever grateful to him for pulling me over after political science class. Thanks, John, I'd say, for believing in me.

Fate never allowed that conversation to occur, but John's sudden death shocked me into a new way of life. I vowed to carve away time each day or each week or each month to stay connected, say thank you to the people in my personal and professional lives. I stayed true to that promise and know that John would be proud of my commitment to others. In fact, I know he's up there watching, still pushing me to shine.

John gave me my start and mentored me throughout his life. He also made me a better person and educational professional. He lives on with these lessons:

- Everybody has a talent. Dedicate yourself to finding yours and be your best.
- Believe in yourself.
- If you're going to achieve something, give it your heart and soul.
- Take time throughout your life's journey to thank those who made a difference.

Mr. Ira Light

Once I had my college degree, I jumped into the job market with high hopes and a foolproof strategy for employment. Although I had dual certification in physical and special education, I focused my applications and interviews on special education, where my prospects seemed brightest. Openings for gym teachers were few and far between back in 1977.

One week into the new school year I landed a job at Cornwall Elementary School. Principal Ira Light met with me on the first day, offered his support, and helped me gather all the materials that I'd need in the weeks and months to come. I had 12 students and a paraprofessional, and Ira stopped by the room each day to see that everything was running smoothly.

It was a busy first year of teaching. A few months later I attended a meeting for Special Olympics and decided to volunteer. The next thing you know I was coordinating the entire event involving athletes and teachers from at least 40 school districts in Berks, Lancaster, and Lebanon counties. This was a huge undertaking, and I relied on my communication and logistical skills to organize the event and raise funds. I wanted Ira to be proud of me and hoped that he'd be impressed with the event, which attracted a couple hundred students.

You see, Ira had a way of making me go the extra mile. On many occasions during my teaching career, Ira would approach me with requests that seemed to match the energy and passion of an eager, young teacher. I dressed up like Santa Claus, helped with the school play, pitched in with PTO fundraising, and my personal favorite, masqueraded as Spiderman. The school needed Spiderman for an assembly, and Ira told me he'd supply the outfit if I'd play the part. And sure enough, when Ira said he would do something he came through. Suiting up in that Spiderman outfit was a treat in itself, but I had to put my modesty aside—it was skintight. Luckily, I had a mask and made the most of my superpowers that day. I ran around the school and played Spiderman, and nobody ever knew it was me.

After doing these jobs Ira would always follow up with a personalized note. Whenever I received one of them, I sat and reflected on my effort and my actions. Ira's notes were sincere, and his pat on the back ignited a desire in me to do more. Decades later I found myself writing notes, just like Ira did. In fact, I believe these notes are one of my trademarks as a school administrator.

Ira never gave up on kids. When one of my students was habitually late, Ira customized a plan to gradually help him change his ways. The student arrived about 15 minutes late each day, but Ira's plan helped him ease into punctuality. If he was 15 minutes late today, tomorrow Ira suggested the student arrive 14 minutes late. The next day, the student arrived 13 minutes late. Then 12 minutes late the day after. He believed in all students regardless of their school performance, disability or bad habits.

It was no coincidence, then, that during my second year of teaching Ira embraced William Glasser's 12 Steps to Discipline, a popular educational philosophy in the late 70s. I remember all of us being trained in this process that encouraged teachers to seek alternatives to corporal punishment to address unacceptable behavior. Ira was firmly against paddling any student, and he would urge teachers to give students the benefit of the doubt. He wanted us to be inventive. Try every solution imaginable to help students overcome poor behavior.

His theories were put to the test not long afterward. A student who frequently pushed the limit of classroom rules was, truthfully, driving one of his teachers crazy. At times he even got the best of Ira. As a principal, Ira did his best to conceal his frustration until that one memorable day. He was suddenly called to Mrs. Miller's classroom, and Ira had to walk by my room on his way. A few minutes later I saw him return, wrestling with the student—literally dragging him down the hallway. What a scene. I never saw this side of Ira.

By the end of the day I thought it would be safe to talk with Ira about the incident. He vented his frustrations in a way I never saw before. His normal levels of patience and understanding were depleted. I suppose I couldn't help myself, but I asked him why he didn't use William Glasser's technique. I was trying to be funny, but I did not have tenure at the time. How would Ira react? Would I be fired or would he scold me for my attitude? He immediately broke down laughing and said, "How would you like to be a principal and deal with discipline?"

And so the seed was planted. Maybe I should be a principal like Ira. He was a down-to-earth person. He was a teacher just like me. We all observed Ira helping teachers put up bulletin boards, covering classes, taking recess duty, and doing everything he could to make morale high. We were very lucky to have a principal like Ira Light. He was well respected throughout the county and especially at Millersville University, where he taught many courses for teachers. Ira's leadership style was to spoil teachers as much as he could, and I knew I wanted to be just like him.

As I worked toward my principal's certification at Temple University, Ira decided to make me his apprentice. I became head teacher at the school, which enabled me to conduct fire drills, set up schedules for teachers, introduce speakers for assemblies, plan in-service programs, and assume principal duties in Ira's absence. After working with Ira for seven years, we agreed I was ready to move on.

I asked Ira for a letter of recommendation, and I cried as I read it. He wrote so many nice things about me. After applying for several jobs, I landed my first principalship in the Red Lion School District, and I'm certain that letter carried a lot of weight. During the final interviews, administrators from Red Lion visited me in action at Cornwall to get a better understanding of my duties and what the school was like. One year after I was on the job at Red Lion the superintendent told me that my elementary school was an exact replica of Cornwall. That comparison was a huge compliment for me and Ira because Cornwall was a place that put great emphasis on the children and their successes.

Ira and I stayed in touch throughout the years, and I'd always get one of his notes when he learned of something positive going on in my life, such as receiving my doctoral degree.

When Ira became ill and was hospitalized in Philadelphia years ago, his family discouraged visitors due to his deteriorating physical condition. This was difficult for me because it brought back the painful memories of not being able to say goodbye to my first mentor and friend Dr. John Spears.

I couldn't imagine being deprived of another farewell with a friend who had been so instrumental in my personal and professional growth. I called the hospital, defying his family's wishes. I had just become the superintendent at Tulpehocken and wanted Ira to know. To my surprise I was connected immediately.

"Is this Eddie?" he said into the phone (Ira was one of the few people in my professional career who called me Eddie). I told him my news and promised that I would serve as superintendent the same way he served as elementary principal. I promised him I would help teachers, support teachers, and treat them the same way he treated me.

As we concluded our brief phone conversation, Ira said that he loved me. A few days later he was gone, and I cried the same way I cried when I heard the news of John Spears.

Ira was a field general among the foot soldiers, and his work habits, demeanor and respect for teachers

set the tone for my style as a principal and school superintendent. His practices became my credo:

- Support classroom teachers and always go the extra mile for them.
- Be willing to perform the same task that you ask a teacher to do.
- Send positive notes to staff members and students. It really demonstrates the value you place on individuals.
- Never give up on a student or staff member. Keep trying to make a difference and don't quit until you taste success.

Dr. William Starr

When I first met Dr. William Starr, superintendent of schools in Lebanon, PA, I was really impressed with his stature and disposition. Bill is about six feet tall with white hair and a great, broad smile. As soon as I saw him I knew I was in the presence of a strong and confident man who was going to help me grow as a professional.

I was just completing my second year in the Red Lion School District when I learned that the Lebanon School District was looking for an elementary principal. At first, I had no interest in applying, but I was curious about working in an urban school. Red Lion is rural, and I believe it's important to see and experience different sides of education—poor, rich, urban, rural, suburban. Going to Lebanon posed no problem to me because I was raised outside the city. It was a familiar place, and in no time it seemed like I was packing my bags and heading toward a bigger school.

Bill eventually assigned me to two elementary buildings, Henry Houck and Harding Elementary. I was also tasked with planning an in-service program for Lebanon and Lancaster counties, the first of its kind for a gathering of this magnitude. Since I learned that I was going to work with my former boss and mentor Ira Light on this program, I was confident and determined to make this in-service a huge success.

The first year more than 800 people attended. I did most of the planning at the district office, so Bill received progress updates and details regularly. I was proud of the work, and Bill offered lots of positive feedback. I knew he liked what I was doing, and after a while I believe I became his fair-haired child. He started calling me "Eddie," only the second person in my life to do so. He told me that Dr. Richard Sherr, assistant executive director of special education, got upset about this, but I didn't care. Personally, I loved the attention and laughed that anyone would get upset over this.

As a first-time principal, I made mistakes, and Bill put me in my place quickly. Once, while investigating an after-school incident on the playground, Bill phoned me to get details. I wasn't there because I had left early without telling him I'd be gone. The next day he called me to his office and instructed me to run my building correctly. In the future, he insisted, I needed to ask or inform him when leaving early. I got the message, and it never happened again. That episode taught me that it was possible to be friends with an employee while also being a firm boss. To this day I believe I execute that lesson well, and I learned that from Bill.

By 1986 I was principal at just one school—Harding Elementary—and I ran a tight ship. Bill told me that parents had called to complain about the way I was dismissing students at the end of the day. I did not want to disappoint Bill in any way, so I asked him if he was upset. He replied with that smile of his and said, "Did you think of alternatives?"

"Yes," I replied.

"Then I support you."

I learned two more lessons that day. Bill said that if he didn't get any complaints about me, he'd be concerned. On the other hand, too many would make him worry. I finally understood that I was not going to please everybody. My second lesson was this—if I was truthful with Bill, I'd always have his support, which is not always the case with administrators in public schools.

Bill appreciated my work and trusted me enough to help him plan an administrative retreat at Lebanon Valley College, a three-day event with all the administrators and department chairpersons from the Lebanon School District. Bill asked me to conduct a 45-minute presentation on effective telephone communication skills. I was delighted and enthused about this opportunity, especially since I was a bit of an expert on the topic—I was constantly on the phone with parents.

Things were going pretty well until the day Dr. Harry Zechman, director of the Lancaster Lebanon Intermediate Unit, appeared at my door. He wanted me to apply for a job at the IU conducting staff development programs. I interviewed for the job but wasn't really interested. A few days later I got a call from Dr. Lee Rhodes, the assistant executive director of the IU, who said that I should really consider coming to the intermediate unit. He made a strong case for the IU and the job and convinced me I should make a move.

How was I going to tell Bill? I greatly respected Bill but at this moment I greatly feared Bill. My news would be unexpected, and I worried about his reaction. I remember going to his office and telling him that I was leaving the district. Bill was not a happy camper, and I'm sure after I left he was on the phone to his good friend Harry Zechman. Bill planned to hold me the 60 days by contract and believed that Zechman could wait.

Before my departure I attended a new-teacher induction program, and as Bill was making introductions he told the group that I was "going to retirement land." You see, Bill believed that I'd encounter much less stress at the intermediate unit than I would as principal in an elementary school. I understood Bill being upset because, truthfully, I would have been too. Bill insisted that I continue planning the county and in-service programs, and Dr. Zechman agreed. It was the least I could do for someone who did so much to cultivate my administrative experiences and leadership skills.

There's not a day goes by that I don't think of Bill or the lessons I learned under his watch:

- You can have a positive rapport with administrators and staff, but you also have to be the boss; sometimes that means making tough decisions with your employees.
- Even happy, positive people experience difficult times, and when Bill was serious, it would be best to stay out of his way. Sometimes fear and respect go hand in hand.

- Be truthful. Always. Bill appreciated my honesty and taught me that when you give people enough rope they will eventually hang themselves. Lying catches up with everyone.
- Bill taught me to communicate with the school board regularly. Make weekly reports and include the good and bad. If a crisis occurs call or send an email to each member. Bottom line: board members never want to hear news secondhand. And they don't ever like surprises.

Dr. Lee Rhodes

I started at the Lancaster Lebanon Intermediate Unit on Columbus Day, 1987, an appropriate date for someone who was stepping into unknown territory at work and at home. I had a new job and an infant son born just a few weeks before on September 1. Change and challenges were everywhere.

I vividly remember my first day on the job. I met with Lee, who served as Assistant Executive Director, and IU Executive Director Harry Zechman. They wasted no time giving me my first official assignment. I was to create an alternative education program for students in Lancaster County, and my supervisors hoped for a quick turnaround. I needed to be ready to present the program to school superintendents by November.

While I began my work, Lee asked that I shadow him for the first two months on the job. One of Lee's favorite lines was, "You need to get to know the lay of the land," and his suggestion was extremely beneficial to me. One of the first places we visited was the Hempfield School District, where we conducted a middle states evaluation. Everybody there knew Lee, respected Lee, and asked him for advice. I quickly learned that Lee was an outstanding instructional leader and resource for his peers throughout the region and state.

Those first weeks flew by. As I shadowed Lee I continued to put together the alternative education program. I presented on schedule, received favorable comments, and then learned I'd be going to Nova Scotia. Lee was sending me to a principals' program that would be the basis of training I'd provide for the elementary and secondary principals in our service area. He also told me to prepare for a trip to Charleston, South Carolina, so I could receive training in cooperative learning. It soon became clear that Lee wanted me to become expert in the latest, most cutting-edge topics in education and teaching. I knew that it was important to listen and do anything Lee Rhodes told me. I had so much respect for him that I began looking upon him as my second father. It seemed appropriate because Lee always had my best interests at heart.

My presentations became more frequent, and the annual, three-day Lebanon Lancaster IU in-service program grew to include some 1200 people. Meanwhile, our IU was becoming recognized as one of the best in the state, all due to Lee's vision. While Lee worked hard to advance the IU, he provided guidance and direction to me personally in curriculum and instructional practices. Unlike my old job as principal, I now assumed the role of an instructional leader—someone well versed in the latest teaching practices—rather than the manager of a building.

During our heyday I helped Lee organize a study council for our superintendents to be held in Washington, D.C. We had the best consultants in the country attend, but one of our presenters got mixed reviews. Although she did an outstanding job, this particular expert was straightforward and dry—no sense of humor whatsoever. The feedback indicated that the audience appreciated her expertise but not her personality. Lee's comment to me was, "I guess the next time I should get a comedian." He and I still joke about that to this day.

Lee was a bit of a news junkie. He was known to read everything in the newspaper, and it would not be uncommon for him to ask, "Did you see the article in the paper the other day regarding..........?" I always seemed to miss the stories, so each day I began looking for articles that he might mention. Sometimes they could be the tiniest thing in the newspaper, but my knowledge of the world outside of school grew tremendously, which was important.

Because I would often travel to different parts of the country for consulting, Lee would frequently offer his expertise about my destinations. And, his scouting reports were always accurate. He also seemed to be well connected. Here's a typical example. Lee might say, "Do you know the guy you met the other day? His cousin's uncle and my best man at my wedding were roommates at Millersville." Other times he might say, "Interesting story about the guy you met in Philadelphia. Did you know that when he was in high school he scored 56 points in a basketball game?" Lee had a story and a connection to everybody I met. My goal was to always outdo him, and to this day I'm still trying. I'm not sure if I'll ever catch up.

Lee was well respected, and in many ways reminded me of legendary Penn State football coach Joe Paterno.

During his career Lee was asked numerous times to apply for superintendent jobs but never acted upon any of the offers. Joe, too, was approached for many head positions in the NFL but never budged from the PSU campus. Both men were the best in their class and always at the top of their game.

Meeting and working with Lee changed my life. His direction and guidance provided a wealth of knowledge for me to use as an assistant superintendent, consultant, and eventually a superintendent:

- Keep current and well-schooled in the latest educational techniques and research. My instructional leadership clearly was as a result of Lee.
- Be quick. Lee taught me how to think on my feet when it comes to educational issues.
- Take that extra step. Even when I thought I had a great program in place at the intermediate unit, Lee would stretch me to do more. He brought out the best in me.

Dr. Joseph McSparran

After five successful years at Lancaster Lebanon Intermediate Unit, I realized that I missed having my own building and serving as its administrator. Around that same time Dr. Joseph McSparran, assistant superintendent at Manheim Central School District, encouraged me to apply for an elementary principal position. The district was looking for a strong leader to oversee the consolidation of two country schools into a single elementary building. Joe's news intrigued me. It was thrilling to believe that I could be a part of local history as the district opened a new elementary school, and the prospects of working with Joe, a familiar face from my days at the IU, made this a tempting proposition. I applied for the position, got the job, and the challenge began.

Joe and I shared a similar work ethic and personality and connected immediately. He offered historical background on the schools about to be shuttered, which provided insight for our communications with staff and parents. These schools had been part of their lives for decades, and change to this degree would be stressful. After many meetings with Joe, teachers, and community members, we successfully opened Doe Run Elementary on September 9, 1992.

Not long after the opening Joe and I collaborated again for the building's open house and dedication. Although I felt comfortable working with Joe, our work was always under the scrutiny of the district's head administrator, Dr. Lewis Jury, whose dominating management style could stop a project in its tracks. The stressful work environment drew Joe and I closer as friends and colleagues.

The first year of Doe Run was a huge success. Teachers got along with one another; students, parents and the PTOs were happy. During my first year as principal, I received my doctorate degree, and Joe was one of the first to congratulate me. He took me out for dinner and gave me a copy of Webster's Desk Quotations that I have on my desk to this day. Inside he wrote, "Congratulations on the attainment of a personal and professional goal. Joe, November 1992." Joe made a big deal out of this moment, and it gave me goosebumps to realize he shared this milestone with me.

Later that year Dr. Jury announced his retirement, and the school board immediately hired Joe as his replacement. Joe had a reputation for being dedicated, hardworking and having strong ties with the community. Not long after, Joe encouraged me to apply for his old job—assistant superintendent. Despite some questions from the board, Joe convinced them that I was the top candidate. I was hired, and Joe and I continued to work together and had a positive first year.

During that second year, however, Joe and I weathered many storms. We coexisted with a micro-managing school board and a meddlesome former superintendent who routinely exerted his opinions on school affairs. Joe and I attended 6 a.m. personnel meetings and then board meetings later the same night. Board members were intrusive, demanding to know why and who we hired. The teachers' association believed there was a lack of communication from Joe and me and requested regular chat sessions. Joe and I also paid the price for living outside the district, which the board discouraged.

Things went downhill quickly. Later in the year Joe and I were involved in a discipline matter that incited a good deal of community protest. It was only my second year in that role, but I remember each day Joe gave me words of encouragement. He said we were doing the right things. I believed him and kept my nose to the grindstone.

Then one day a board member who supported our work and decisions asked Joe to go for a car ride. It was an unusual request, and I found it a bit mysterious. As a new administrator I was scared because I did not know what the future held for me or Joe. After their conversation, Joe called me into his office and said, "If you have a chance to get out of here, do it." The look on Joe's face was grave. He had dedicated many years of service as a high school principal, assistant superintendent, and now superintendent to the Manheim Central School District. He was respected and admired by community members, staff and students.

I continued to work with Joe until there was an opening in the Lebanon School District. I was hired back as an elementary principal with my former mentor Bill Starr. I was sad to leave Joe, but not Manheim. After my departure, the board bought out Joe's contract, and he became a successful professor at Kutztown University. Manheim Central continued to experience upheaval in the years that followed. It was somewhat comforting to know that the strife was not our fault but just the way things were done in Manheim at that time.

Looking back at this time in my life, I probably was too young to become an assistant superintendent. Without the support of Joe, though, things could have been far worse. Through it all Joe McSparran led by example. He always took the high road and believed in me without question.

Into each professional life a little rain must fall. I was lucky to be with Joe when the clouds gathered:

- Remain confident in front of the people you lead. If you don't, they too will lack confidence.
- Stay the course and ignore the distractions.
- Consider the ripple effects of change before you act. They will exist.

Dr. Woodrow "Woody" Sites

I have known Dr. Woody Sites since 1987, the same year that I started working at the Lebanon Lancaster Intermediate Unit. Woody was Superintendent of Donegal School District, and though I never worked directly for him, he played an important role in my career.

As a curriculum and staff development specialist, I would attend monthly superintendent meetings held at the Lancaster Lebanon Intermediate Unit. Sometimes my supervisor, Dr. Lee Rhodes, and I would make presentations to the group, and two of my earliest were dedicated to an alternative education school and an effective teaching technique called cooperative learning.

After creating the alternative education program, Woody approached me and told me that I did a nice job. He even said that he would support a program like the one I designed. I was flattered that a superintendent would give me this type of positive feedback. As an individual who works hard to satisfy people, Woody's response helped my self-esteem as a newly-hired employee.

At the next monthly superintendents' meeting, I made it a point to be around Woody, just to get to know him better. Each meeting after that Woody and I would engage in conversation, and I felt that a friendship was in the making.

Each spring the IU would conduct a retreat for superintendents. I attended these retreats and often pitched in as facilitator. Our agenda was focused on setting goals for the following academic year and determining how the IU could assist school districts. After participating in the monthly superintendent meetings, I noticed that the retreat guest list included many head administrators who were the most outgoing and jovial in nature, yet serious and focused when it came to getting the job done. At times it appeared to be a good old boys club, but I was happy to be a part of this fraternity of educators.

On the day of the retreat, we'd form a caravan in Lancaster and make several stops before reaching our destination. One of the stops would be at Mendenhall Inn, located near Longwood Gardens, where we'd engage in food, spirits, and good conversation. On one of the trips I sat across from Woody. By this time it was obvious that we had clicked and enjoyed each other's wit and sense of humor. I remember the night when he looked at me and said, "Hey, you. You are a good guy, and you have a bright future ahead of you." I suppose Woody liked my personality and disposition, and by the third mixed drink he may have been feeling their effects. Nevertheless, his comment was sincere, and I was beaming to hear his positive words. To this day Woody still says, "Hey, you" when he's about to give me advice.

My relationship with Woody and the other superintendents continued to grow as we met at events or educational settings where I was making presentations or facilitating discussion. I'm proud to say that our IU offered excellent in-service programs, and I believe I was in the right place to hone my leadership skills. Listening to and watching these talented individuals was very important for me. It was like a personalized training seminar on leadership. I would often focus on Woody when he spoke and interacted with other superintendents. I believed his open, direct style of leadership matched my own.

During my stressful days at Manheim Central, where I worked as assistant superintendent, I reached out to him for advice and remember asking him to lunch. I explained that I was scared to leave my current position and apply for an elementary principal job back in the Lebanon School District. I remember exactly where we sat inside the restaurant in Manheim when I asked Woody what would happen to my career if I left. He assured me that it wouldn't be damaged. In fact, he specifically mentioned that the most fun he had in education was being an elementary principal. He said I was young (age 40 at the time) and would do an outstanding job. Someday, he assured me, I'd be an assistant superintendent again. Taking the next step to a superintendent, he said, was inevitable. I believed what he said and trusted his advice. He must have had a crystal ball because that is exactly what happened. Woody assured me of this plan and gave me the confidence to pursue the principal job in Lebanon.

Over the years, Woody would often discuss rural schools and their funding with other superintendents. Little did I know how much that topic would affect my life, because just as Woody predicted, I became a superintendent, this time in a rural school district. I was hired as superintendent of Tulpehocken Area School District in 2009, and my path crossed Woody's again, this time with the Pennsylvania Association of Rural and Small Schools (PARSS), where he worked as Assistant Executive Director. The primary function of PARSS is to lobby for fair funding for rural schools. I got appointed and served for five years as a PARSS board member and attended board meetings four times a year in State College. Now, I serve as Executive Director of PARSS and will continue to work with Woody on legislative issues and travel for presentations.

Woody, you have been a wonderful mentor, friend and yes, 'dad.' (I'm his adopted son, you know). I know you will continue to tell me to walk first, then run.

I continue to learn and laugh with Woody and know he'll serve as a source of sound advice and educational vision for many years to come:

- When tensions are high, use humor to break the ice. For example, get out of your seat at a superintendents' meeting, walk across the room and confront a peer in a charming way.
- As you continue your professional journey you will meet individuals from various backgrounds and experiences. Keep an open mind with everyone you meet. Listen when they speak. You'll gain valuable knowledge and insights.

Dr. Jon Rednak

Dr. Jon Rednak was the superintendent at Solanco School District during my time at the Lancaster Lebanon Intermediate Unit and part of a group of savvy administrators who I believed was in the know. He attended monthly gatherings for superintendents and was the type of person you wanted to hang around with before the meeting started—especially when he was with his buddy, Woody Sites, another one of my mentors. The two of them were characters.

I was always impressed with Jon's easy disposition and how he championed kids and staff. At each of his own board meetings he would recognize students for their hard work, talents or achievements. He sent birthday cards to staff, which is where I got the idea to call all employees and sing, "Happy Birthday" while I served as superintendent at Tulpehocken. I did not work for Jon but learned a lot from him.

Jon owns a second home in Tampa and frequently drives to his place to escape the cold. When my son, Brixton, decided to attend graduate school in Tampa, I asked Jon if I could catch a ride with him to deliver some essentials to my son's apartment. He agreed and off we went, along with Jon's huge bag of peanut M&M's and lots of Dr. Pepper.

By the time we got to Tampa, though, I had eaten most of his candy and screwed up the air conditioning in his new GMC Acadia. Jon was stressed because he couldn't imagine something like this going wrong. I desperately searched through the owner's manual but couldn't find answers. I then called GMC for help. Remember, we were heading south, and Jon was driving along getting hotter and hotter. Then, it started to rain. Things became a tad tense, and we were getting nowhere.

Finally, Jon said, "Ed, there is a switch in the backseat. See if it is on or off." I checked and told him it was off. It should have been on, obviously, but I must have accidentally bumped the setting while reaching around for those Dr. Peppers. It was that simple. Thanks to me, I ate all his M&M's and put us in a sauna for 45 minutes. He probably wanted to drop me off in Georgia. The trip, otherwise, was great and filled with conversations about life, school, and his years as a superintendent.

Like Woody Sites Jon, too, was an officer with the Pennsylvania Association of Rural and Small Schools (PARSS), and my involvement with PARSS threw us together. In 2013 we were attending the annual PARSS conference in State College. The conference traditionally opens with a golf tournament, and Jon and I played in the same foursome. We approached a par three hole, and Jon teed off first. He took a big swing and hit the ugliest line drive I've ever seen. It looked like a ground out in baseball. The ball hit a bank in front of the green and then disappeared. As we got closer to the green, no one could find the ball.

I thought it may have rolled all the way to Pittsburgh, as terribly as it was hit.

Someone in our foursome peeked inside the hole—we didn't know where else to look—and there was Jon's ball. Miraculously, he had a hole in one! That was the first time I witnessed a hole in one and still can hardly believe it, considering how ugly it looked off the tee.

It is a general rule that after a hole in one you retire the ball and the scorecard to your man cave at home. But not Jon. He teed off with it on the next hole and hit the ball into the woods. Lost forever.

When Jon retired from Solanco, he began conducting superintendent searches for an Iowa-based company called Ray Associates. One day in 2014 Jon asked me to help him do a search, and I gave him a quick yes. I liked the idea of spending more time with Jon as we collaborated on work that I thought sounded pretty neat. Our first search was in Millville, Pa., and it was exciting to be involved in a process that would identify a school official who would make a difference in the school and community.

Jon and I teamed up two more times, and I learned a lot from him about conducting a superintendent search on a national level. A footnote about our teamwork: Before school board presentations, we would devise great plans. Jon would say, "Now Ed, I want you to tell the board how we are going to interview the candidates." But then Jon would go ahead and tell them how we were going to interview the candidates. Then he'd turn around and say to me, "Ed, tell them."

I really couldn't get too upset about Jon's timing or his presentation skills because he soon had to put up with me after I broke my foot in 2014. He tolerated my scooter and my long rehab schedule and would get me food, open doors and carry my materials whenever we were on the road. He was a great caretaker.

Jon was a model for my leadership style and opened doors to exciting projects and future endeavors:

- Take time to build morale among staff; recognize student achievement.
- Create a sound public relations strategy to promote educational programs, facilities or concepts.
- Keep board meetings productive and efficient.
- Undertake every superintendent search with a serious sense of mission and the highest level of integrity. Respect the process. The person you choose can make or break a school or community.

Mr. Joe Bard

When I joined the board of the Pennsylvania Association of Rural and Small Schools (PARSS) back in 2009, Joe Bard was already serving as executive director. Little did I know that he would become my next mentor.

At one time Joe was the PA Deputy Secretary for Elementary and Secondary Education and was still tightly wired into political circles in Harrisburg and Washington, DC. Pennsylvania governors going back to the 70s consulted with Joe on educational issues, and he's particularly well known for his advocacy of outcomes-based education that took hold in public schools during the 1990s.

As Joe and I traveled to State College for PARSS meetings, I would listen closely to what he had to say. The round trip was four hours, so this was my chance for some carpool class time. I had the utmost respect for Joe's knowledge and experience in education policy, and he always seemed to have the inside track on events happening in Harrisburg. Joe ended each PARSS meeting with updates from the educational front in Harrisburg and at the federal level. He was often in Washington to brief high-ranking officials, such as the Secretary of Education, and in some ways reminded me of my first mentor John Spears, who was another political insider with lots of good sense and connections.

Joe was a force. With his knowledge and credentials he met most of his PARSS goals without much opposition from anyone on the board. Not too many people were going to challenge Joe Bard. He was articulate and part of a powerful network of politicians, and knowing that he was an advisor to many governors made you pause before questioning him. In fact, I thought it would be crazy to challenge Joe. But I did it anyway.

During one of our meetings we were discussing the upcoming governor's race between incumbent Tom Corbett and challenger Tom Wolf. Joe agreed with other political analysts about the race revolving around education. One of my colleagues on the board suggested that PARSS set aside money to fund a debate dedicated entirely to the topic of education. Joe's response was unexpected. He immediately said no. End of discussion. Joe also vetoed a much less consequential suggestion for musical entertainment during a PARSS conference. Someone suggested a band composed of retired administrators perform, and once again Joe said no. I challenged both these decisions and called him out on it at a board meeting, perhaps the first person to do so in a PARSS setting. We shared our views, and afterward I told Joe that others have opinions that need to be considered too.

Later, at our annual conference, WGAL political analyst and professor of public affairs at Franklin & Marshall, Dr. G. Terry Madonna, was our featured speaker. Madonna now serves as a Senior Fellow in Residence at Millersville University of Pennsylvania. He is well known for his political and pre-election surveys. Those of us attending could have listened to him to all day. When he opened the floor to questions, I decided to get his opinion about a possible debate between Gov. Corbett and Wolf. Like all the other political pundits, Madonna agreed that this election would focus heavily on education. He thought my idea was wonderful, and I found myself beaming from ear to ear. I finally got one on Joe. Afterward Joe approached me and asked me what I was trying to do. I acted the innocent.

I believe that PARSS is a well-respected organization because of the experience and expertise of its board members, but some of the senior members won't be able to serve forever. People like Joe and Woody Sites and Jon Rednak won't be easy to replace, but for PARSS to continue its mission representing rural schools in Harrisburg, there needs to be a plan for the future. Without PARSS, rural schools have no voice in Pennsylvania, so board members started to address the transition of personnel and leadership.

By spring of 2015, the plan was complete and presented to the board. It recommended that an assistant executive shadow Joe for the next few years. Ideally, that person should be retired and have the time to be with Joe in Harrisburg, meeting legislators and learning the ropes of policy development. The board approved the plan, and I am proud to say I was appointed to that position effective July 1, 2015.

Prior to this announcement Joe and I traveled to Penn State to meet with school superintendents. During that visit I asked Joe why I got the new job with PARSS. His answer surprised and encouraged me. Joe said I was the first individual who challenged him, and he liked that. He also assured me that I'd be a quick study and continue the important work of PARSS with energy and new ideas.

Dr. Ed Albert

During the past five decades I've been on the receiving end of advice from mentors. Now, for this final chapter, it's my turn to offer some guidance. I've broken it down into three distinct essays: "Roots," "High Spirits," and "Facing the Music."

ROOTS

Let's start with my Dad.

When I became a first-time administrator, I remember my father saying, "Never forget where you came from. You were a teacher first."

The comment resonated and certainly echoed what Ira Light pounded into me. As an administrator, Ira routinely covered for teachers, and the feedback he received from staff was positive. One day, I knew, I'd make it a point to do the same.

It began early in my career as an administrator. I'd cover classes and occasionally teach lessons. Returning to the classroom kept me grounded with the kids, and it was a reminder of the profession I left behind.

The more classrooms I visited and the more classes I taught, the more rewarding it became to me. While working in educational administration, I opted to take vacation days to begin a dual career in consulting. There's no way I wanted to be hired as a consultant and then tell teachers I was in the classroom years ago. I'd be unrelatable, and they would believe, rightly, that I was out of touch.

Through the years that followed, active classroom visitations became a trademark for my job as an administrator and my part-time consulting business. That's where I'd hear many teachers remark, "My administrator never walks into my room," or "My administrator taught so long ago, he/she has forgotten where they came from." I never wanted that said about me, so wherever I worked I made certain a particular number of teaching days was required in each contract.

I was selective about where and when I taught. I can assure you it was in classrooms where I was at ease with the curriculum. It's a safe bet it was not biology, chemistry or higher-level math classes. I popped in elementary rooms and various middle school and high school classes where I knew my background would be a match. I went out of my way to identify the most difficult classes or classes scheduled at the end of the day in order to demonstrate how to win over students and model strategies I lectured on in my consulting sessions.

Those experiences were tremendously worthwhile, and I routinely left with a sense of shock and awe—shock at how much preparation is required to produce in-depth lesson plans and awe at the effort required to create the wide array of modifications and accommodations for all types of students. "How do they do it?" I frequently asked myself while exiting a classroom.

I can report that the staff and students loved having an administrator come to the classroom to teach. The connections were endless, and the experiences kept me aware of the environments and challenges teachers face each day, each period. I never forgot where I came from.

HIGH SPIRITS

Throughout my career I've prioritized building and maintaining morale among staff. What makes my list of suggestions different from others is that each item has been road tested in schools with tangible results. To duplicate my positive outcomes, good deeds and thoughtful gestures must come from the heart. Be visible. Be personable. Get out there and demonstrate your interest. Actions must complement the work you do with teachers, staff and community members each day. Here's what worked for me:

Push yourself to send at least 500 positive notes throughout the year.

Visit each teacher daily. YES, it can be done! Staff members love the interaction...kids do too.

Call teachers on their birthday, even on Saturdays and Sundays. When the spirit moved, I sometimes sang, "Happy Birthday."

Get to school early and greet teachers as they arrive. Maybe you can help carry materials into their room.

Learn something about each employee and show an interest in that particular fact. Recognize what they do and celebrate their accomplishment.

Take recess duty for teachers, especially in the winter.

This will give you an opportunity to get to know the kids, and it will also save you time reacting to recess discipline issues. Kids rarely misbehave when you are watching them on the playground.

Place a carnation on each person's desk with a note saying, "We are going to make a positive difference for the students we serve. I am here to support you."

If you are a new administrator, obtain staff photos from the previous year and study the names of the teachers. Everyone's impressed when you address them personally before meeting them for the first time. During those early days of employment at a new school or district, I began a habit that I continue today. After a first meeting or classroom visit, I jot down the person's name on an index card along with a few other distinguishing facts. Perhaps they mentioned family members or a unique pastime or project. I'd record it all and study the cards. Next time we met, I was prepared for meaningful conversation.

During teacher appreciation week, go all out for the ENTIRE staff. Provide extra time for staff members to eat their lunch. Recruit a retired music teacher to play piano in the faculty room. Spruce up the tables with linens, too.

Send faculty agendas out a few days before your meeting. Mark discussion items with an asterisk to give staff a chance to prepare. Keep meetings to 30 minutes. Max.

Observe teachers starting the second week of school and have the observations completed before April 15.

May is a crazy month for educators and observing teachers late in the school year is neither effective nor appreciated.

FACING THE MUSIC

If you're a school administrator—or hoping to be one someday—I want you to consider a radical idea to achieve your district's goals more swiftly while dramatically boosting your accountability with staff.

At the end of each academic year invite all faculty, staff and fellow administrators to evaluate YOU. Anonymously. And then share the results with everyone in your district.[1]

Yes, you'll need pluck. And maybe some protective armor at first, but trust me. I'd never suggest you do something I haven't experienced myself. It's a good thing to do.

Introduce your survey with a statement of purpose. Make it clear; you seek constructive feedback for the purpose of personal and district-wide improvement. Then hit the send button so the questionnaire lands in every employee's email box. Explain that all results will be compiled, reviewed and shared later.

Michael Leister, former junior high house principal at Tulpehocken, was a nonbeliever at first. In fact, he thought I was out of my mind. "I had never heard of a superintendent doing this before," Mike said, "but what was most shocking was that he was going to share the results with everyone, which he did."

The eleven survey questions ranged from "Do you think the superintendent is approachable?" and "Do you trust the superintendent?" to "Has the superintendent supported you in crisis, classroom setting or project?" After the last question leave plenty of blank spaces for comments, too.

From the perspective of an administrator, it would be great to say that all of the surveys came back with glowing remarks about the wonderful job I was doing, but honestly, some of the comments and ratings hurt on both a professional and personal level. Three respondents called me a bully. Another one accused my frequent appearances in the hallways as politically motivated because I failed to greet each employee in my path.

I didn't blow off those negative outliers. In fact, it was essential I give thought to those perceptions, even though I may have disagreed. Had I not reflected on the feedback, I would have disowned those employees' points of view. Naturally, bruising comments caught my attention at first, but after a few weeks I formed a new attitude about them—instead of getting hung up on the negativity, those comments transformed into opportunities for growth.

School administrators tend to evaluate their leadership abilities by looking through their own lens, and that perspective is often skewed. The surveys helped me see how I was perceived in the eyes of the staff.

By the way, I'm happy to report that not all the results were negative. There were some who thought I walked on water. The truth, I suspect, is somewhere in the middle.

[1] Albert, Edward; Davis, Barbara, Bottiglieri, Jason, Full Circle: Making the Most of 360 Principal Evaluations, The Pennsylvania Administrator, February, 2014

ACKNOWLEDGMENTS

Although I've created a memoir of mentors in this book, there are several others who deserve acknowledgment for their roles as guardian angels, cheerleaders, soul soothers.

To Salem College coaches Harry Hartman and Larry Blackstone, you helped me during the critical transition years as I adapted to college life and athletics. Without your guidance and encouragement, my journey in education may have veered desperately off course.

Later in my career there was Evelyn Fox, a board member serving the Tulpehocken School District. She was honest, open, and pulled no punches.

Finally, a special shout out to former Pennsylvania Secretary of Education, Eric Haggerty, who urged me to share my stories with a wider audience.

And Linda Miller, thanks for the editorial guidance and occasional nudge. To all, a giant thank you.

The ultimate act of thanks is to pay it forward; therefore, proceeds from each sale of *Mentors Matter* will be donated to St. Jude's Children Hospital.

Other Individuals Who Played a Positive

Role in My Success as an Administrator

While mentors helped me attain goals and begin new professional experiences, there were numerous other staff members, fellow administrators and board members who made my day-to-day life more efficient, more productive, and more satisfying. For every pat on the back, kind word, and gesture of support, I remain forever thankful.

Cornwall Lebanon School District
- Dr. John Menser
- Mrs. Karen Light
- Mr. Floyd Becker
- Mr. Larry "Ike" Eisenhauer

Red Lion School District
- Dr. David Ginder
- Dr. Ivan Shibley
- Dr. Dale Reinecher

Lebanon School District
- Mr. William Kuntz
- Dr. Fred Richter
- Mr. Robert Bowman
- Mrs. Lisa Beard
- Mrs. Lisa Kiessling
- Mrs. Linda Pepley
- Mrs. Terri Davis

Lancaster Lebanon IU#13
- Dr. Harry Zechman
- Mrs. Sharon Althouse
- Dr. Doug Stark
- Mrs. Kelly Shenk

- Mr. Ed Golden

Manheim Central School District
- Mrs. Mary Adams
- Mr. Bob Daecher
- Mrs. Pat Paules
- Mrs. Hazel Nestleroth
- Mrs. Marsha Parido

Eastern Lebanon County School District
- Dr. Richard Nilsen
- Mr. Howard Kramer
- Mr. Doug Good
- Mr. Jack Kahl
- Mr. Mike Simmons
- Mrs. Tina Kunder

Tulpehocken Area School District
- Dr. Barb Davis
- Mrs. Bonnie Benfer
- Mrs. Cindy Jenkins
- Dr. Jason Bottiglieri
- Mr. Tom Kowalonek
- Mr. Mike Leister
- Ms. Lisa Kiss
- Mr. Scott Klopp
- Mrs. Trudi Bux
- Mr. Glenn Dunkleberger
- Mr. Rob Neiswender
- Mr. Mike Debakey
- Mrs. Mimi Shade
- Mr. Chuck Warfel
- Mr. Brian Boland

ABOUT THE AUTHOR

Dr. Edward Albert worked as a teacher, elementary school principal, assistant superintendent, and superintendent of schools during his 38 years in education. He currently serves as the Executive Director of the Pennsylvania Association for Rural and Small Schools, advocating for more than 240 member districts on policy, funding and educational issues. Dr. Albert also serves as consultant to schools across the country and conducts superintendent searches for districts throughout the state of Pennsylvania.

Dr. Albert frequently presents at local and national educational conferences, contributes to The Pennsylvania Administrator, a publication from the Pennsylvania Principals Association, and advises school administrators on long-range and strategic planning, board retreats, and keynote speeches.

No matter if it's before a single superintendent or an audience of teachers preparing for a new school year, Dr. Albert is best known for his down-to-earth personality and relatable presentation style. In case you need more proof: Dr. Albert served as a school administrator for 31 years and always included a stipulation in his annual contracts requiring that he teach five full days each year. His objective was to never forget his origins as a classroom teacher.

www.alberteducationalconsulting.org

www.ingramcontent.com/pod-product-compliance
Lightning Source LLC
Chambersburg PA
CBHW061810070526
44586CB00024B/2799